Reasons Why Youth Don't Give A Damn Anymore!

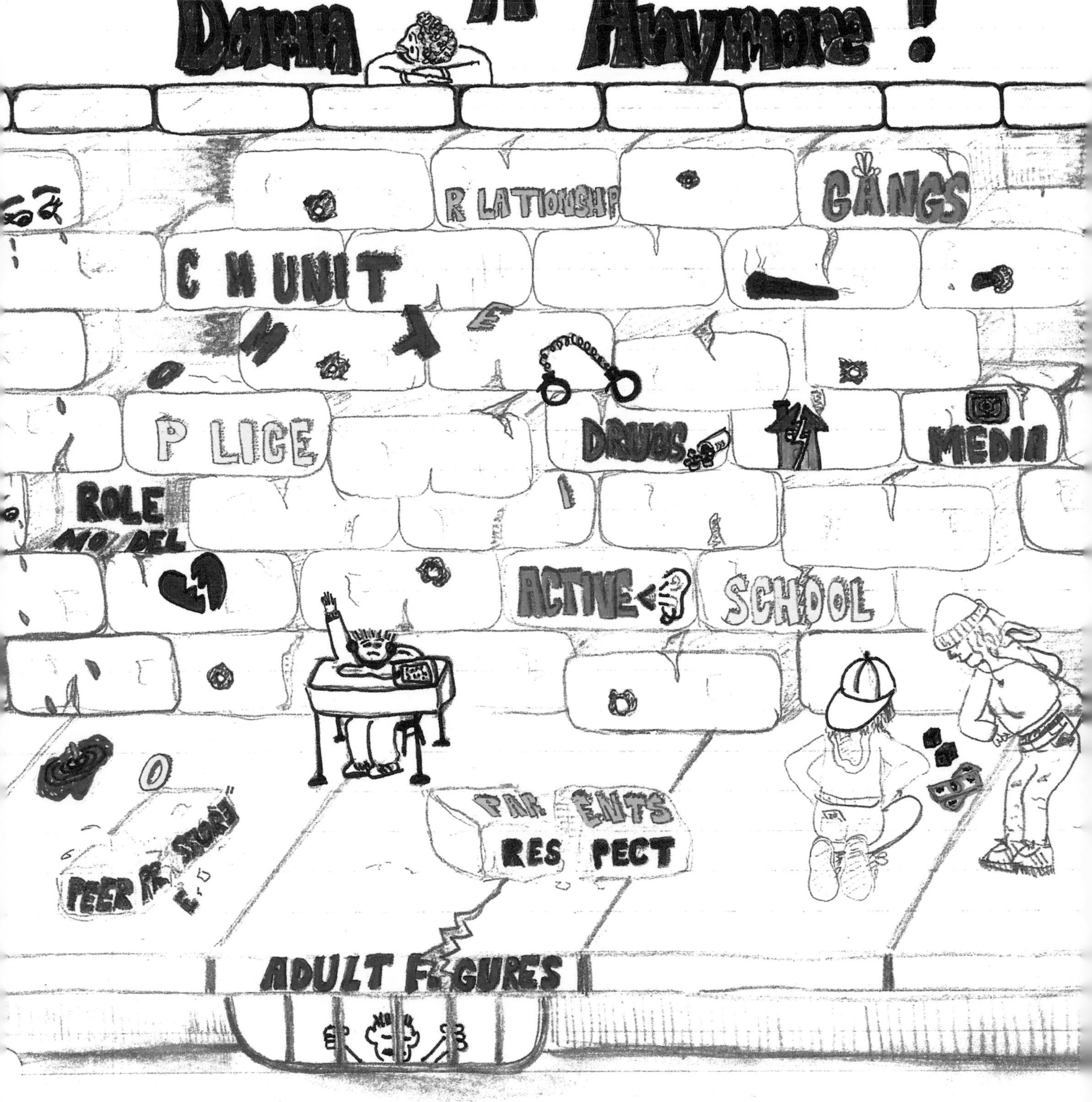

BARRY WOODS

To order additional copies of this book, contact:
Xlibris
844-714-8691
www.Xlibris.com
Orders@Xlibris.com

ISBN: Softcover   978-1-6641-3644-1
        Hardcover   978-1-6641-6235-8
        EBook   978-1-6641-3643-4

Print information available on the last page.

Rev. date: 03/10/2021

This book is dedicated to my Nana, Mary Scott Cook and my cousin, George Ross.

A special thank you to The Dream Team: Patricia Woods, Alexis Woods, Debra Wilson, Dennis Carter, Jon Hoch and Allan Houston.

TABLE OF CONTENTS

> Today's teenagers are more disrespectful than ever before and are getting worse due to the lack of respect that they have for themselves, families, parents, teachers, males, females, peers, and education.

> Adults don't feel that they should have to justify their actions to young people, but expect young people to justify themselves to them all the time.

> Todays' parents are younger and have less life experience; this is due to many different factors. Often times it's because they are still in the process of raising themselves and don't effectively understand how to manage their emotions. We live in a time where it seems having a baby is more of a fashion statement then a life-changing moment.

> This is the attitude of our most challenged young people, who struggle to get ahead or get a fair shake (as they see it) in the game of life. The school system is not set up to support them, only to maintain them. Or, to do just enough, so it can't be said that they aren't doing anything.

> Regardless of whether or not we agree as adults, we have to respect the way the young people see things as their reality.

Mr. Woods' Tool Kit

Mr. Woods' Hard Facts for Young People

Introduction

"REASONS WHY YOUTH Don't Give A Damn...Anymore!!" is the forbidden text, the taboo, the new playboy that you read in the bathroom during your 15 minute break. It's in your face reading! No short cuts, no pillow talk, more like a straight shot of Bacardi 151 with no chaser. Young people today are more visual and media-driven than ever; as adults we have to watch everything we say and do at all times!

What inspired me to write this book? The first reason is to open the minds of influential adults who are involved in the lives of young people. Parents, educators, police, advocates, probation officers, mentors, role models, employers, community leaders, parents, counselors, youth workers or anyone who works closely with young people or will have a direct impact on the growth and development of young people. Young people learn by watching you, the way you treat them, and how you treat others. We need to open the door to the hard conversations and address the issues we don't like to address as adults. Yes, dealing with little Jonny may be tough, but he learned his ways from the adults around him, so they need to be held accountable too. Yes, police and teachers are authority figures and young people need to show them respect, but they must be respectful as well. Everyone must remember that respect is a two way street. Respect has to be earned; you don't just show up and get it!

Along with addressing the grassroots issues that affect positive and productive youth engagement, this book also offers tools for self-improvement and professional development for adults working with young people on a personal or professional level. As well as those adults playing a supportive role in the lives of today's young people as mentors, big brother, or big sister. There is no way that this book should be just another book to sit on the bookshelf in your office or home library. It should serve as a primary reference tool for educators, youth advocates, probation officers, mentors, police, parents, role models, counselors, youth workers, and community leaders to help build stronger relationships with young people. Educators and agency supervisors can use this to work with their staff. Teacher workshops, Youth Advocate trainings, Counselor trainings and Police trainings can all find use of this book to help them be more effective in their line of work with young people. That's right! This is gut check time! If you read this and do nothing, you're part of the problem, especially if you are working with young people.

Lastly, I would like to start a dialogue with community and faith based agencies to create a, "grassroots", in-your-face, parenting curriculum. The job we have as parents is tough because we struggle to balance the impulse of when to teach and when to protect. By protecting we satisfy our, "Hero Complex", the feeling of gratification for saving the day around whatever ever the issue maybe. On the other hand, when it comes to teaching, the instant gratification comes much slower. It takes time, months or even years, for young people to understand values, principles, how to apply them in life, and the reason why you say, "NO." This is a critical piece of the process because that helps young people learn how to manage life as well as how to deal with life altering situations.

Parents should read and role play some of the scenarios with their children. Let them speak freely and openly in the process; you'll be surprised at what you hear and you might learn something too. For the parents who feel that your child doesn't have these issues, "You're part of the problem!" Adults who are in young people's immediate circle are the most influential people in their lives, you have more of a direct effect on their development than you realize.

On a broader scale, the goal of this book is to heighten overall awareness of the need for adults to step up and be appropriate role models for young people and allow them a better chance at being successful in life. What are the real reasons that we are compromising the growth and development of our young people? Selfishness, greed, self-entitlement, putting today before tomorrow and the future of those who will be the ones managing tomorrow. We are killing the spirits of our young people and losing them to drugs, teenage pregnancy, the streets, crime and, worst of all, ignorance. In 2008, according to the 129th Edition Statistical Abstract of The United States out of 196 million people surveyed for US Census ages 25 to 34 years old: 11.9% or (40,146,000) had no high school education, 28% graduated high school but only, 41.6% perused post-secondary education the other 58.4% did not. In the same year 78.7% of high school students graduated but 63.1% also dropped out of high school. Of the 78.7% who graduated 15.7% were unemployed and of the 63.1% who dropped out 25.8% were unemployed. These are low income jobs we are talking about here, positions paying no more than $15.00 per hour. For some reason, our young people today are struggling to push themselves to the next level. I would like to see more serious dialogue and commitment from "us" as a society. There needs to be more communication and alternative support for low-income young people who are unidentified and seem to get lost in the process.

I have written this book to be objective, generate conversation, make adults working with or around young people question themselves and the systems of support, education, community, parenting, policing, and how they affect the development of our young people. We need to stop looking for our own personal gratification when giving young people guidance about life. That is what we are supposed to do! It's just like in the streets, your big homie's are supposed to look out for you and guide you so you don't get bagged by cops or caught slipping by your enemies. That's what's needed from educators, community members and parents; give that proper guidance and let it go. Don't get caught up with looking for the thank you or the pat on the back right away. It will come over time, maybe even years later. Things are not right and need to get right! The underlining factor is to change the culture of our young people by being more accountable as adults and role model appropriately. Thank you for your time and enjoy your reading.

Respectfully Yours,
- Mr. Woods

1. **Lack of Respect** - Today's youth have a serious lack of respect for: themselves, family, parents, teachers, males, females, peers, education, educators, clergy, and adults who hold positons of authority. The foundation (home) is where all basic life instructions and values are taught. Who to respect? Who not to respect and why? How to act? How not to act? Along with who it is important to behave in front of, showing respect to your elders and adults in general.

2. **Adults don't show or give respect but expect to be respected** – Today's adults need to take a new approach. The, "Do as I say, not as I do" parenting role model approach that has been used since I was born, is not the same now. Nor does it hold the same principle value as it did then. Due to today's parenting styles and the fact that parent today are a lot younger. Today's parents don't have enough life experience, and are not fully developed mentally or emotionally themselves.

3. **The Media Effect** – Through social media regardless of misuse and abuse, young people experience instant gratification, global acceptance, instant reaction, and peer acceptance without any buffers. This presents a false reality of acceptance for young people, that they accept as their reality and sometimes view these examples as true paths to success or ways of life. Movies, videos, music, TV shows, news channels are baby sitters.

4. **Disengaged Parents** – Today's parents because of their age (16 to 37) get tired of being parents because they have missed so much of their own life. It is important in human development that we experience all phases of development to successfully move to the next level in life. Disengaged parents usually have gaps in their development that need to be addressed.

5. **Negative Norms** – Norms are learned behaviors. In our society, we have many negative norms that we teach our young people every day. We hope that they do not pick them up or repeat them. These behaviors range from lack of respect for elders, peers, drug use, the use of foul language, hygiene, how to dress, the importance of education, just to name a few.

6. **Enabling Adult "I Want To Be Your Friend"** – Adults think they help kids by doing things for them, getting them out of trouble, not holding them accountable, and not having them face consequences.

7. **School Systems** – Schools are not set-up to deal with the effect society has on the student's attitude about education as well as the neglect that they receive at home. The school system is a 10 month Band-Aid compounded by the verbal abuse and rejection young people receive at school from teachers, administration, and peers on a daily basis. Students do not feel supported or like they can get support from their school if labeled at-risk. This may cause them to be embarrassed to ask questions for help when struggling. Budget cuts taking away after school activities, community resources, and in school support.

8. **Peer Pressure** - Today's peer pressure for young people is different from the 80's and early 90's. Parents, teachers, counselors, clergy, and anyone working with kids need to understand, be very aware, and respect how today's youth see peer pressure. We have to respect the perspective of their reality as they see it, not as we see it!

9. **Adults Talk More Than They Listen** – Adults needs to realize one thing, we may know a lot of things but we do not know everything as we like to make it seem sometimes. Learning to listen is a hard thing for us adults because that means that we have to be quiet and not say a word. Have an open mind, and really make an effort to understand what a young person is saying. As the authority figures of today's young people, it's important we understand their views, ideologies, and emotions.

10. **Gangs** – The most influential thing besides social media affecting young people's attitudes is around family, life, and education. These are fueled by triggers in three domains: school, home, and community. For example, common triggers at home would be one of the following: 1) Parents condone it because they live the gang life style or were a product of it. 2) Parents do not believe that their child would be involved with these kinds of things.

11. **Parents Are Poor Role Models** – Parents do not realize the effects their behavior have on young people. Some excuse it as being acceptable because, "we are adults", wrong! Our actions, words, and behavior around our children help shape our children! We need to remember that before we do or say things in their presence.

12. **Cowboy Cops** – Some police officers are a big community trigger for teenage attitudes about life, future and education. This is not to bash police officers because I do support their mission but as they say one bad apple can spoil the whole bunch or spread like cancer. Police need to understand that the interactions they have with young people can effect their future, education, and family development.

<u>NOTES</u>

BARRY WOODS

How do I meet young people where they are?

» Accept their reality for what they see it as, not what you feel it should be.
» Don't try to change their values; try to enhance them and allow them to change things on their own.
» Allow them to be expressive; don't worry about correcting them right away. You can always double back and create a teachable moment. The goal is to get them to, communicate freely and honestly without thinking of consequences.

CHAPTER ONE

"The Lack of Respect"

RESPECT IS A value recognized by actions that transcend through communication between people. Respect is also a feeling, which communicates fairness and ownership of your feelings and the right to express those feelings without compromise. Respect is the foundation for everything in life, both good and bad. How respect is handled or managed depends on the value of respect that you place on the issue or situation at hand.

Today's teenagers are more disrespectful than ever before and getting worse due to the lack of respect that they have for themselves, family, parents, teachers, males, females, peers and education. This chapter will explain the lack of respect in each area and how it affects the lives of teenagers today.

FAMILY

According to the Webster Dictionary a family is a social unit, a group of people sharing common ancestry. This means that the family is the primary place where behaviors are learned and passed on, generation after generation. Today's family units are very different than those of the early 80's and late 90's. Think about it. Mom and Dad work now, and single parent homes are more common now, more than ever. When was the last time you had dinner as a family, watched a TV show with your kids or even sat down and talked to them about their day? I mean, your family is the one group of people who should accept you as you are and love you unconditionally, no matter what! Instead, today's families are the first to alienate you from the family if you fit the category of a social outcast such as: homosexual, date outside of your race, drug dealer, convicted felon, etc. Families don't even have common values like they used to like, trust! Some families have secrets within the family that they hide from each other and you expect the children of that family to be trusted and/or trust worthy... How? Where will they learn that value of trust from? How will they know what that value looks like if they don't have it being modeled at home daily?

Without a system or common routine, there is no reason to respect the family unit. For example, having dinner every night at 6:30pm is routine and should be respected by the family as dinnertime. However, if everyone eats whenever they want via the microwave and takeout, there is no dinnertime to respect! It's more like lunch at work, eat as you go, relax if you can, a quick hi & bye and I'm gone. Now how can you call yourself a family when you have nothing in common and you don't spend enough time with each other to know enough about each other's lives because everyone is so busy? So busy that you can't check in with each other or when you try to have a conversation the phone rings and the conversation is never completed. Too busy to check report cards, so teenagers sign them on their own just like they do detention and suspension slips because they don't get the sense that education is important from their family. Even worse, your child gets a good grade on a test, makes the honor roll, receives an award from his/her teacher or has an issue about a teacher and/or another student that they need to really talk to you about, and the family is not there. The thought process of a young person is this. If young people don't feel that their family cares about what they are doing, then their reaction is, "why should I care about them, what they want me to do, or what they are doing; nobody cares about me." Things like this create that, "I Don't Care Attitude" we see from young people today. Everything starts in the home, with the family; so, if your family works as a strong unit, has solid values, and positive routines, then you can expect to see that behavior in the youth of that family. On the other hand, if your family doesn't work as a strong unit, does not have solid values and/or practices negative routines as values (like ones mentioned above) then you can expect to see that behavior in the youth of that family as well.

Young people learn the most by what they see and hear, because they grasp things much faster auditorily and visually. What they see and hear daily is their reality and are the same things that make them sensitive or insensitive to the things that happen in life around them and/or to them. Overtime, as young people develop, they carry forward what they learn. In a form of reflection like a mirror in a lens, so our guidance in this process is key. In the words of Ms. Wilson, *All young people have a road but they need a map.* Think of it as if you're building a house. The house is only as good or as strong as its foundation. If the foundation is weak eventually the house will fall down, because the cracks in the foundation will continue to get bigger. They can repaired; but, that takes a lot of work! And frankly speaking, from what I've seen, families are not willing to work that hard anymore. How can you expect a child to be respectful if they don't come from a respectful family?

PARENT(S)

Parent(s) are teachers, teaching life to their children. Parents are their children's heroes, enemies, best friends and role models; but, first you are parents. I think parents forget that parenting is a job. From the day of your child's birth until they become a self-sufficient adult, that's the assignment! **NOT TO RAISE THEM JUST TO THE AGE OF 18, 21 OR 25 a self-sufficient adult**! Don't pawn your unfinished business on the taxpayers or add weight to another member of your family or the community, "**STAY COMMITTED AND RAISE YOURS!**" As my mother used to say, **"IF YOU ARE GROWN ENOUGH TO LAY-UP AND MAKE A BABY, BE GROWN ENOUGH TO RAISE ONE!"** - *Sandra Woods*

Parents have to remember they are the picture of respect for their children. That picture you paint has a major effect on them. Parents need to role model respect for their children. Think about it, your kids see you every day, even when you don't think they see you, they see you. Just like you did when you were young… That's right, you were once young, too; you made mistakes, too, right? So, when certain things happen, don't do the **"NOT MY KID"** thing, the only difference maybe that you may have not been caught. On the same accord, you must also remember that your mission is corrective action or proactive action now.

Young people need to see what respect looks like in different settings: home, the mall, at work, in the car, in the street, when you come to school, on the phone, etc. It is important that they see you being respectful in several settings so they can learn how to be respectful in those settings themselves. Let me give you a common scenario that happens in school and something adults never pay attention too.

SCENARIO

Mark is an 8th grade student who is struggling in his reading class with Mr. X. He has been missing homework, not completing class projects, coming to class late, cutting classes and has been both disrespectful and disruptive during class. Detention slips were sent home and haven't been returned signed, messages have been left at home and work for his parents, but there has been no response. When Mark talks to his parents about school, he always blames the teacher, stating that the teacher doesn't like him and he's always being picked on by him. Due to the grades that he received during the first marking period, a parent teacher conference, was scheduled with Mr. X, Mark and his parents. The day before the conference Mark is being disruptive as usual so Mr. X removed him from class and assigned him detention that afternoon. Mark turns around before he leaves the room and says, "I don't like your stupid class anyway; you wait until tomorrow! My parents are going to curse you out, and I'm not going to your stupid detention anyway", and slams the door. Now, when Mark gets home, he runs to his parents and tells them, "Mr. X tried to give me detention today, for nothing; I think he's upset about the meeting tomorrow. I told you he don't like me."

Fast forward. So it's the next day, you're getting prepared to go to the school for the meeting and your feeling some type of way because it's your child that they are talking about who is the problem. As the meeting goes forward, you start to get upset because you don't like what you're hearing about your child. Next thing you know you're attacking Mr. X and disrespecting him in front of your child and before you leave, you say, "Well, you never liked him anyway. I don't want him in your class anymore."

WHAT DID YOU JUST DO???

You just showed your child how to deal with frustration and disempowered his teacher by agreeing with your child through the actions you showed and the statement you made, "...Mr. X is picking on him and doesn't like him." You just made your child feel they were right and, even worse, that you both are on the same page. Yes, I understand you're human and you got naturally frustrated when hearing negative things about your child. So that makes it ok, right? **"NO!"** A common assumption adults make is, **" IT'S OK BECAUSE I'M AN ADULT; YOU DON'T DO THAT!!"** Yeah, right! **WRONG!** How are you going to do something that you alway tell your child not to do right in front of them and expect them not to do it? You are their parent(s); they learn what to do and what not to do by watching you! Ashamed of yourself and not knowing how to respond or what to say, your apology for your behavior is McDonalds or new IPhone, because you feel like shit about your behavior. **"NO!"** You're sending the wrong message! You just celebrated the fact that you just disrespected your child's teacher. Not to mention, you just showed your child how to deal with a frustrating situation and did a very shitty job at it, role model!

THE AFTER EFFECT:

Now, when your child returns to school the teacher is their least worry or concern. They also have a different tone and attitude now when dealing with that teacher (**FYI:** and other adults, including yourself) because they now know that the parents don't like the teacher neither? Well, that's what they saw. They feel that you agree with them, about the teacher picking on them because that's what they heard you say. Unless you come into school and apologize for your behavior in front of your child, so they can see what it looks like, you can't expect them to be respectful in school (or to you). You have not shown them what respect looks like in a school setting, how to respectfully deal with adults or how to handle frustration respectfully! Then, the next day they disrespect the teacher in school, similar to the way you did in the meeting, in front of the class or any other adult for that matter. When you get home, you're upset about your child's behavior, yelling and scream about how you told them about their mouth and not to disrespect their teachers. They say, "But you know he doesn't like me..." You say, "Regardless, you don't do that; I'm getting tired of telling you...." They're going to come back and say, "Why not; you did," you're going to get more upset, yell even louder, spank or punish them. **(Or, maybe even all three, depending on how bad of a nerve they hit!)** For what? Because your kid called you out! They only know what you teach them, through your words and your actions... literally, through your words and your actions. So, in essence, you punished your child for following your example and telling you the truth about your own actions. Hmmm...do you think that's fair? Now you wonder, as the years go on, why your child has no respect for you. If you have shown no principles, no morals, no respect in several areas as mentioned earlier, don't expect your children to show respect, period. Not to you or anyone else, unless you show or have shown them different!

"UNDERSTANDING DOES NOT EQUAL ACCEPTANCE."
- Harron Rahmey, 2002

As parents we have a hard job to do, and we must stay focused on our responsibility as parents and stay involved. I will discuss more later in the book about the severe damage that, "Disengaged Parents" do to the attitude of young people today. As parents, we must be the role model of all role models. We are the ones our children are learning from! For example, when your baby repeats the word, "shit," everyone laughs and says it's so cute, right? Wrong! It's inappropriate and an 18-month old baby shouldn't be saying that. Which means you shouldn't be saying words like that around them! Now, I know we are all human and mistakes happen, little slip-ups here and there; it's understandable but not acceptable, period! End of discussion!

EDUCATORS

Next to parents, educators are the most important and influential adults in the lives of young people today. Just as they learn by watching their parents, they learn by watching you, too. Over 85% of educators are control freaks and never like to admit or accept that they're wrong or can be wrong, which is an entirely different issue within itself. Educators need to step down off their imaginary pedestal and realize one thing, **"YOU'RE NOT PERFECT"**! Yes, you can be wrong, too! Yes, you can be rude, unapproachable, and inappropriate! Yes, you can be disrespectful, manipulative, and spiteful! Yes, the things you say to students can be hurtful and demoralizing! Yes, you can have an attitude or be off one day due to personal stress! **WHY?** Not because you're an educator, but because you're a human being dealing with the everyday pressures of your world, **just like your students**!

See, the problem is that educators contradict themselves by their actions daily and have a role as an authority figure. A good authority figure is a person who commands respect by their actions, presence and the way they treat others. At the same time that they command respect, they give respect to the people they oversee and deal with on a daily basis.

WHAT DOES RESPECT LOOK LIKE IN AN AUTHORITY FIGURE'S ROLE?

As an authority figure, to gain respect from people you may manage, oversee or deal with on a daily basis, the first thing you must do is commit to being fair and honest with yourself and the people you manage, oversee or deal with on a daily basis.

FAIR & HONEST

As an authority figure, the people you manage, oversee and deal with on a daily basis dictates your respect from the masses. To be a fair and honest person of authority, there are some key skills that you need to develop and always be conscious of. The first is the ability to listen. Not to be confused with **hearing**, is the ability to open your mind, be empathetic and non-bias to what you hear and still render good judgment based on facts. Regardless if you have been or are being disrespected, or listened to yourself. You must make a decision based on fact, not feeling, and that's an issue that educators struggle with. This is mainly because of what I like to call the, **"YOU OWE ME,"** complex that educators develop due to the effort they put forth to a young person in their life and educational development. The reality of it is that a young person doesn't owe you anything except respect! Not a thank you, an appreciation card, nothing! No matter what you have done to support them through their education and life development. If they choose too, yes, it's a beautiful thing and it makes you feel appreciated like the bond you have with the young people you touched is so strong. But what about the young person who choose not to stroke your ego, but they are productive in class, have you stayed with them for extra help, allowed re-takes and curved test scores to help their grades? Again, **"THEY DON'T OWE YOU ANYTHING,"** It was your choice to be an educator. If you wanted to be celebrated or praised for your efforts, then you should have chosen a career in politics. It's your job to go all out and support youth in completing their education and preparing them to be productive in life so they can contribute to our society in a positive way as self-sufficient adults.

Next is being able to "ACCEPT" opinions from everyone peers, elders, and young people regardless of them being right or wrong. Do you believe everyone has a voice? Not to mention the constitutional right of, "Freedom of Speech," which includes everyone, even young people, like it or not. The ability to accept is a skill that allows you to see everything in black and white, leaving out the gray. As an authority figure, you have to role model righteousness, which means you have to be able to admit your faults as well. Adults have to remember that admitting their faults is not a knock or a put down. It bridges a gap that is naturally formed between young people and adults. It turns you into a human being. It lets young people see that you are not a robot or perfect; you make mistakes and bad decisions, too. Just because a person is younger then you does not mean what they have to say is not important, may not be true, or that you can't learn from it. They have feelings just like you do! So, if it hurts when someone steps on your foot, then why wouldn't it hurt if you stepped on theirs?

The third and most important piece of being able to be "Fair & Honest" is the ability to accept "FEEDBACK." The hardest and most powerful skill you can develop when dealing with young people is being able to take in their feedback. Not just because it's coming from a person other than your peer, supervisor, spouse, family member and a person who is younger than you are; but because what's being said is likely negative and is likely true. It's just no one ever had the guts to say anything to you until now. More importantly, you are allowing them to know that they have a voice, you respect their feelings, and allow them to see that you're human just like them. Everyone does something to wrong people at least once in their life and you are no different. Being able to own up to your mistakes, change your behavior and keep respect is a challenge, because you expose yourself through feedback. The biggest thing to remember about taking in feedback is that you're not the only person with an opinion. People have a right to their own opinion (which doesn't have to agree with yours), just like you have a right to speak or state your opinion and be heard. Like it or not, so do other people, no matter what race, religion, or age they are.

SELF-RESPECT

Today's youth have such little self-respect for themselves it's crazy! They are so quick to disrespect and or kill one another for little to no reason, for something as small as a bump in the hallway, crowed party, street, or sidewalk. Not to mention the effect the media has on their peer groups, which helps to influence the development of cliques and gangs. Along with the extra added negative bashing they receive from family, teachers and peers (jockeying for position or cool points).

Now, before we go any further, let me explain something. This is not to point the finger at anyone; but, as an individual, you have to understand the effects of your actions on others, especially young people. Now, I know young people can be very disrespectful and push your buttons to the limit, like you did your parents, teachers, and other adults (both professional and non-professional). Did they give up on you?

The majority of you would say, "NO," but for those who say, "YES," do you remember how you felt? The object is to elevate and educate our young people, not to help destroy them and encourage negativity or self-destruction.

This means when adults (parents, teachers, family members, neighbors, community members, police etc.) call young people stupid, little shits, bastards, or say things like, "You're going to be nothing in life," "You're a lair," "I give up," "Your ass is going to end up in jail just like your brother," or "You ain't shit, just like your father," it contributes to the negative mindset of today's young people. If these things are said behind closed doors, it is even worse, because that means the adults' implicit bias is clouding their judgement when approaching young people. Even though none of us wants to admit it, we all know adults who talk to young people like this. Some of you reading this right now could most likely be one of those adults. Some may call it the, **"TOUGH LOVE,"** approach for today's youth. Not so, **"TOUGH LOVE,"** is negative feedback backed by positive reinforcement and empathic follow through. The average adult says these things out of anger and frustration without thinking (just like young people do), but your behavior is for a reason and is supposed to be understood right? Why, because you're an adult? I don't think so! As an adult, it's your turn to teach now! Remember, you're always teaching in all situation and scenarios, as mentioned earlier and sometimes you are going to make mistakes. Some bigger than others, just like young people. Understand something, people. Today's youth take what you say to heart, and society just makes it even more vivid.

Today's struggling young people have an attitude that can't wait to say, "FUCK YOU," and are motivated by money, power, and respect. So, what are you doing about it? Are you part of the solution or part of the problem? Are you turning your back and acting as if it is not there because it's not on your street, house or in your neighborhood? Maybe you are in denial and think that your child is the only child in the universe not exposed to any of the world's natural evils. They float around in a soundproof bubble, listening to tapes of your voice and instructions on how to live their life and they never disobey you. Or maybe you feel like you have done enough?

If you had your children between the ages of 15 and 19, dropped out of high school, or didn't complete college, because you had to work to support your family. Now you're 35 to 39 years of age, and you feel like you're 65 because you started your adult life early. You feel you've done enough as parents and you want to enjoy your life a little and your child's issues are in the way of that. The irony is that your mother and father or another close family member practically raised your child, because you were still young and running around going to parties and out on dates. The most one-on-one time you had with your child was at family gatherings, hanging outside with the girls, playing ball at the park with the boys, sleeping, watching movies or going to the mall. Therefore, you really just started being a fulltime parent.

Young people today need to feel self-worth and believe that they have self-worth. That's why they cling to today's social media and gangs, because that gives them a sense of of belonging and power. Young people today at risk for gang violence believe to be respected is to be feared and feel they can get that from being in a gang. They feel appreciated and loved when they look fresh, or the top athlete in the school, or the flyest guy/girl on the street, all blinged out. That makes them feel accepted! Self-worth should be taught through family and societal values, not power and flash. Why? Because power and flash can always be taken away, but strong values are rooted into your foundation; so, when all else fails and everything breaks down, you can rebuild from a solid foundation.

<u>NOTES</u>

How do I meet young people where they are?

» Allow behaviors to happen so you can understand where they come from and what the triggers are.

» After open communication has been established, start to offer advice and give corrective action. This allows young people to maintain the feeling of self-control and they don't feel like they are being told what to do or how to act. This creates a window for a teachable moment—a more intimate level of engagement that allows young people to receive feedback and not feel like they are being attacked.

NOTES

CHAPTER ASSIGNMENT

Objective: To build positive self-worth and improve the lack of respect in today's youth.

Goal: Focus on having positive communication with young people on a daily basis. Remember, everything you do is a lesson – every action, statement, movement etc.

Assignment: Keep a log or a journal of your interactions for a year. Log conversations, situations, all advice given, positive statements and keep notes on the change in behavior. Track no more than 3 young people at a time so you can really focus on the development; if you have kids at home, start with them first.

Feedback: Email all questions and feedback to Reasonswhyyouthdontgiveadamn@gmail.com

BARRY WOODS

How to discipline with empathy:

» Listen.
» Share your own stories about making poor choices and facing discipline: this helps open the "TRUST BUCKET" with the young person.
» Separate needs from wants; supply them with needs only. Use their desire for what they want to build value within their behavior. So they understand how they impact their own development and set limits.

CHAPTER TWO

"What's Good for The Goose is Good for The Gander"

"Adults (Parents, Educators, Community Leaders, Mentors etc.) are the biggest
role models or influencers that young people have today." – Mr. Woods

SOME OF US feel that being an adult means that as long as you are under the age of 18 the motto is, "Do as I say, not as I do." This is the classic contradiction in communication between young people and adults. Mainly on the part of the adults, because we like to be in control, don't think we can be wrong, and the majority of us are thick headed or do not like to listen. Adults don't feel that they should have to justify their actions to young people, but we expect young people to justify themselves to us all the time! Then, when young people choose not to justify themselves to us, they're viewed as being disrespectful? **THAT'S BULLSHIT!** By you not explaining your actions, you're assuming young people have some computer chip inside them, programed not to allow adult actions to influence their own. It's not just disrespectful, it's unsupportive to their development.

Part of being an adult is having the ability to explain your actions and use them as teaching points to help spread wisdom to our young people. This process is a major part of their social/emotional development by helping young people connect the dots. It shows acceptance, responsibility, and humility; but, most importantly it lets young people know it's ok to make mistake, as long as you learn from them. We need to lose our image of perfection, the superhuman complex that adults do no wrong and bring ourselves back to reality. We need to leave ourselves open for questions that allow young people to point the finger at us and say, "Well you did it, too, so how can you tell me not to." Adults today send mixed messages by saying one thing and showing the behaviors opposite of what they say. This is an unhealthy pattern and is going to have a major effect on society in the future if we don't start to change our thinking.

SCENARIO

Lisa and her 12-year old daughter, Nicole, are going to the mall to do some shopping on Saturday. They go into Old Navy to pick up a few things and are on their way out of the mall. While exiting the mall, Lisa collides with another female customer. Lisa is exiting the wrong way, through the entrance door. The woman says, "EXCUSE YOU!" Lisa continues walking, brushing her bags against the woman's leg, turns and says, "EXCUSE ME! BITCH YOU BETTER MOVE YOU SEEN ME COMING OUT!" The woman replies, "THIS ISN'T THE EXIT DOOR AND NICE WAY TO TALK IN FRONT OF YOUR DAUGHTER!" Lisa replies, "WHATEVER BITCH KEEP WALKING, YOU SAW ME COMING OUT FIRST!" Nicole watches in total shock as her mother turns away and they continue walking to the car in silence.

They get into the car, (mind you, Mom has said nothing about her behavior; she didn't say sorry for swearing, nothing), the Fabolous and Neo song, "You Make Me Better," is on the radio; Lisa turns to Nicole with a reassuring smile, to show everything is ok, recites the chorus to her, smiles, and they ride off.

THE AFTER EFFECT

Two weeks later, Nicole is suspended from school for disrespecting her 6th grade math teacher in class. Her mother was called in for a meeting with the teacher and the principal on the day she was suspended about the incident. The teacher explains what happened: "Class was about to begin, as I was making my way through the door and Nicole came running in with Megan and they both ran into me. Megan says excuse me and ask if I'm ok and states she's sorry for running. Nicole, on the other hand, keeps walking. So I say, Nicole, aren't you going to say excuse me and she goes off! "EXCUSE ME… BITCH I CAME THREW THE DOOR FIRST, WHATEVER..!" So, I sent her straight to the office. Now, Nicole can have an attitude sometimes; but, that was just blatant disrespect, and I will not allow a student to sit in my classroom and talk to me like that!

As the meeting continues, Lisa is visibly upset, and Nicole looks down at the floor, ashamed of her behavior and the outcome of the situation. After making Nicole apologize, Lisa also apologized for her daughter's behavior as well and stated that she will also have Nicole write a letter of apology to the teacher during her suspension and they left.

WHAT IS GOING THROUGH LISA'S MIND

I can't believe this girl, talking to her teachers like that! Where the hell does she get off! See she's been hanging around with those fast ass girls at school, trying to be cute! I can't believe she would embarrass me like that! The school must think I'm a terrible mother and she has no home training. I mean seriously, where did she learn to act like that?

THE FLIP SIDE

Adults tend to suffer from convenient amnesia and forget how much of an impact their actions have on young people, especially their own children! The blinding wall of denial that exists with adults, about how their behavior can negatively impact the development of young people is tremendously thick. If Lisa is wondering where her daughter learned those behaviors, she needs to conveniently remember the incident at the mall and then look directly in the mirror.

DON'T ALLOW ANGER TO BLOCK THE TEACHING MOMENT

On the entire way home it was quiet, so quiet the wind whistling through the particularly cracked driver side window just made the ride more intense. Nicole is just riding with her head down. She can tell her mother is very upset, because every time she tries to say something, Lisa barks, "SHUT-UP!"

THE TEACHING MOMENT

As adults/parents, we must remember that we are always teaching in the presence of young people. Lisa is upset about her daughter's behavior, yes. But, she's also showing her daughter the wrong way to deal with being angry and/or upset. Nicole understands that her mother is mad, but does not understand why she will not talk to her. INTERESTING... Think about it? When was the last time you allowed an upset young person not respond to you or tell you to shut up? That would be disrespectful, "RIGHT?" But, ok for adults to do? What we should do, as adults, is communicate instead of dominate. Explain your feelings so young people can understand the actions that follow. Let them know that you're upset, that you need a few minutes to calm down before saying something because of the situation. This type of communication also helps young people understand that you're upset at their behavior and not them, so they don't personalize things and become resentful.

THE BIG "3"

These are the "3" main factors that need to be present in a "Teachable Moment."

1. **Self-Awareness**
   - Were you a positive or negative role model?
   - Look at your physical reaction to the situation, "What Did You Show?"
   - Don't allow your anger to blind you from this moment.

2. **Self-Acceptance**
   - What part did you have in the situation?
   - Were you out of line in some form or fashion or disrespectful in anyway in the presence of young people?
   - Did you accept that you were wrong?

3. **Follow Through**
   - Walk them through the steps of appropriate communication using yourself as an example.
   - Communicate that you are wrong and you accept your mistake.
   - Allow young people to practice the process you show them, along with you.

<u>NOTES</u>

BARRY WOODS

How to discipline with empathy:

» Make examples of everyone; don't play favorites.
» Respect others feelings and opinions but honor the process: ("I agree with you, but the rules say this…") ("I don't like it either, but those are the rules…")
» Explain consequences, even when you're frustrated; remember, you're not the one facing the consequences, the young person is.

NOTES

CHAPTER ASSIGNMENT

Objective: To support young people in communicating in appropriate ways including anger.

Goal: The next time you get upset with a young person, don't block them out of the process. Remember to remain calm and respectful yourself, young people only learn from what we show them—let them know why you're upset, accept your role, explain what they did to make you upset, when you'll be ready to talk etc. Give them strategies and allow them space to work and develop them with you.

Assignment: Keep a log or a journal of your interactions for a year. Log confrontations between you and young people (you must be open and honest for this process to work). How did you handle the situation? Create a grade scale and grade yourself using, **"The Big 3": Role Model, Self-Acceptance, and Follow Through.** Focus on the teaching moment, what is the lesson or the message you're trying to get across? Track these situations as they accrue, and the outcome of your process, to determine what works and what does not. Focus on one situation at a time. If you have kids at home, start with them first.

Feedback: Email all questions and feedback to Reasonswhyyouthdontgiveadamn@gmail.com.

BARRY WOODS

Things young people need to understand... the hard facts about life!

» You don't have to like school, but you must respect and understand that K-12 is non—negotiable.

» Because you have limited authority, you have to play "chess" and show true diplomacy through your ways and actions, especially when upset.

» Being upset and acting out will only compound things, not change them.

CHAPTER THREE

THE DISENGAGED PARENT

"The problem is you have kids having kids!" - Mr. Woods

TODAY'S PARENTS ARE younger and less experienced when it comes to raising kids, which is due to several different factors that do not discriminate. We live in a time where having a baby or being pregnant is more of a fashion statement than a life changing moment. Where females having a, "baby daddy," means you live off Section 8, state benefits and/or child support instead of working. They look at the father as a new wave ghetto meal ticket. For males, this means making ends meet or holding the fam down, being a real man and getting money. Means get your scam game on, find the next "lick", rob someone, rob a bank/store, sell a few ounces of weed or a few eight balls of cocaine on the side, while holding down a full-time gig and/or trying to start your own business in some shady way.

Today's parents seem more concerned with being liked by their children, rather than being respected. As a parent, you have to remember what you signed on for; 18 years of hard labor, non-stop stress, aggravation, joy, pride, teaching, discipline, and a lifetime of love. The problem today is that parents are fine with the joy, pride, teaching and lifetime of love part of parenting. It is the hard labor of dealing with the non-stop stress, aggravation, and discipline part of parenting they struggle to maintain. The job of today's parents is extremely tougher due to the elements of today's society that influence children: news media, television, music, videos, video games, internet access, adult influencers, peer pressure and parents themselves. Parenting is not so textbook and old school like it was in the early 80's and mid 90's. Youth trends have changed! Their images of a hero and what it takes to be successful are different. They place less energy and value in education and respect, while putting more energy and value into their SWAGG, "staying fly" and "getting money." Due to the poverty-stricken society we live in today, we have some young people emotionally supporting families, financially running households, caring for siblings and caring for parents.

These are not priorities for young people, but the bigger issue is that some parents accept it. To add more insult to injury, the average parent today is more immature than the parents 40 years ago. I've noticed over the years, the effects of two essential elements in parent development: **TIME** and **ATTITUDE**. Time is a key factor and has three major components: knowledge, understanding and development. Attitude is a reflection of time. This is key when you look at the long-term effect of pre-mature adult development and how it effects the development of today's young people. Now, I'm not saying that parents don't have other things to deal with in their adult life. I understand. Work, marriage, relationships, death, money issues, co-workers, divorce, bills, taxes, the asshole boss, and the list goes on. What I am saying is this, **"SO WHAT!"** Nothing I mentioned is out of the ordinary of everyday issues that every adult deals with and you feel you should be looked at differently or given a pass, because why? The only thing I can say is this!: If you're an adult who feels you qualify for my new reality show, "ADULT PITY PARTY," send in your audition tapes, because at the end of the day, **"TO DAMN BAD, THAT'S LIFE!"**

Everyone deals with the same two extreme daily struggles everyday: struggles we have no control over and struggles we create. We all want to take breaks at times and very well deserve them, but parenting is a 24 hour, 7 day a week, 365 day a year job and then some. Are you ready to take on all the responsibilities as a parent mentioned above and then some? Depending on the type of parent you want to be, maybe you should not be having children? Becoming a parent is something that we all control; but, the problem is, it's not respected.

Parenting is a privilege, not a burden and needs to be treated that way. Think about it, how is parenting described among parents today? How many times have you heard other parents, including yourself say: "This/These kid's is/are a pain in the ass!" "This little shit makes me sick!" "These ungrateful bastards don't deserve a dam thing!" The crazy thing about it is that these things are said right in front of a young person and said repeatedly. Which brings about another point: **verbal bashing is not tough love**, but that will be discussed more in depth later in the chapter when I talk about the component of time and how it relates to parenting. Adults should view it as an honor to raise a child in the likeness of God and themselves, a gift like no other. To be a part of a child's growth and development over the years for them to follow your advice, adopt attitudes, habits, traits, talents and or mannerisms to help them reach the next level in life is priceless. To raise a child that does well in school and in life is what every parent wants and is something every parent can have; but, it takes work! A lot of work! Work, that will take you being involved when you don't want to be involved, work you are going to have to do when you are tired, aggravated, sick, hungry or just getting off work yourself. Parenting is a tireless mission, filled with ups, downs, highs, lows and not a lot of instant gratification. Some parents' missions are longer and harder than others, but they all are situations, environments, families and lifestyles that young people are brought into. It is our job as parents to make sure that those things don't effect the development of our young people in a negative way by any productive means necessary.

The conflict in this process accrues when parents who have not appropriately developed the **knowledge** and **understanding** of how these elements effect the **development** of young people become parents themselves. Due to their own rebellion against parental structure, authority and education, many of these parents are still working from a disadvantage themselves, be it financially, emotionally, family related or educationally. Now they are asked to be in charge of a life when they don't even have full control or understanding of their own? Again, a situation that a young person is brought into, through choices made by adults who have traits of rebelling against authority, are misguided themselves, have little to no educational background and lack of proper friend and family support; which brings us back to the two key elements in parental development, **TIME** and **ATTITUDE.**

Time, as mentioned earlier, has three components:

1. **Knowledge**

    Defined as, *Understanding acquired through experience*; having been through life experiences is huge factor when you consider being a parent, life teacher or person responsible for the development of the lives of young people. In order to teach, you must have knowledge through things you have learned from your own life experiences; you can teach as you go, but if you do, you need to have tolerance. Too many (young) parents today have not had appropriate role models themselves and are too proud to admit that they themselves need support and a little bit of structure. Some have emotional, financial, and educational struggles they haven't even dealt with, which has stopped them from reaching certain levels of development in their own lives. In order to progress successfully in life, you need to complete certain cycles in your life which require you to have knowledge of certain things in life. You can only learn through experience. If all your life experiences were negative, then that's all you have to draw on (based off the knowledge you have learned from the life experiences that you have had). Not having enough life experience is a common dilemma that many parents find themselves in today!

2. **Understanding**

Defined as, *the ability to comprehend perception*, your actions as a parent are key in this area. The common problem that falls under understanding is action without explanation. This becomes an even bigger challenge for those who try to use the, **"Tough Love"** approach. **Verbal Bashing** and **Tough Love** are not the same and many parents today get that confused (or twisted). **Verbal Bashing** is about power and control, putting another person down to the point that they feel worthless or upset which causes them to respond with violence or some other form of aggression or disrespect. This only compounds the issue, because that kind of behavior from a young person towards their parents triggers a defensive reaction in adults/parents and things continue to snowball from there. It's easy to lose control and have these situations turn into full blown arguments that sometimes get physical or verbally threatening and conclude with the adult feeling satisfied because the argument was won. This does nothing but build more animosity in young people by making them feel shut down in the process, as if they have no voice. **Tough Love** is about giving a young person the hard facts of life backed by principles and values to help build a stronger character within an individual through self-reflection, empathy and accountability. This means having them serve that detention or suspension: allowing them to stay in jail until their court date and not bailing them out! You may find you are crying yourself to sleep some nights because it hurts for you to watch your baby struggle; but, you understand that they need to make better life choices, and at the same time, understand and respect the consequences they must face, due to their actions. Tough Love is not about being that cool parent, the friend that everyone's kid likes. Or, that parent who always gets their kids out of jams because they have that, **"NOT MY KID!"** syndrome. Understanding is a process based on empathy, accountability and supported by the principle of acceptance, best explained by a quote form one of my mentors, Harron Ramey, "Understanding does not equal acceptance." Now, in order for you to truly comprehend this process, you have to have knowledge through experience, education, and observation. Then, you can understand how to apply it to the young persons' life you are affecting, something a lot of today's parents lack. Again, due to the elements of their own personal circumstances, as stated before, but we must remember that the child is brought into these environments.

3. **Development**

The definition is, *to make fuller, bigger, better; to show or workout by degrees*; development is growth, growth through trial and error. The way that you pick yourself up and dust yourself off in life is a key factor in developing character. Character is a key element you must have to effectively support the young people in your life as a parent, teacher, mentor, etc. In my opinion, to properly support young people through development, you must retain this one key element essential for you to be a role model. To be a role model, you need to have what I call, **"The WISDOM JEWEL."** I define this as the ability to identify a teaching moment, role-play real life situations, give detailed explanations of your actions, and explain why you handled the situation the way you did to a young person. **The Wisdom Jewel** is an important tool for parents, along with anyone working with children (teacher, mentors, counselors, etc.) to develop because it allows young people to see things in action by seeing a supportive adult conduct themselves in their environment in many different situations. Situations are old to us as adults, because we have seen or experienced them before and have learned through trial and error, in most cases. This allows adults to break down a situation in baby steps to a young person, because they know what needs to be done or how to respond to a situation before it happens.

As you can see the three components that make up **"TIME"** are very key components and essential to the development of **"ATTITUDE"** of parents/adults. As stated earlier in the chapter, **"ATTITUDE"** is a reflection of time, which is key because the long-term effect of pre-mature adult development has proven to be a primary factor of the lack of positive development of today's young people.

The definition of **ATTITUDE** is as follows: *A manner showing ones feeling or thoughts: one's disposition, opinion, etc.* The key word in this definition is the word, *"opinion."* Opinions are thoughts and views developed over time to help us create judgments, which affect our lives in many ways: how we react to situations, things we say, body language, posture, tone of voice, our ability to teach, our ability to deal with crisis, frustration, anger, as well as our ability to give and receive feedback. If we only see one side of things in life do to the environment we live in; then, we approach life at a disadvantage. Even worse, that attitude is passed on from generation to generation, to the point where it becomes something like generational law. That is, when you hear kids say things like, *"If she says one thing to me I'm going to spaz, she knows I don't like her ass."* As if that is the way to deal with people you don't like that you still may need to communicate with (they could be a teacher, co-worker, boss, someone's mother, father, sister, brother, etc.). Every situation in life requires a different attitude and approach. Being able to determine which attitude and approach to use in each situation is the issue. This depends on what you have in your toolbox as an adult based on your own development and ability to expand on that development, which is a responsibility of every parent, school, community organization, or anyone working with young people. The following scenario will show the importance of appropriate development of Time and Attitude.

SCENARIO

Tracy is a 35-year-old mother who has a daughter in high school, named Michelle. Michelle is a solid student has an average group of friends and has been involved in no more than the average teenage mischief; overall, she is a good kid. Tracy is a college graduate with a B.S. in Social Work and is employed by the local child services agency and is pursuing her masters. Tracy and Michelle have a very open relationship and are able to discuss anything. Therefore, when the issue of sex came up, the debates began. Tracy had Michelle at a young age, but the road was rough and she was lucky. In her line of work, she sees young girls fall through the cracks every day! Regardless of the fact, she would support her daughter and make sure she finished high school, college and was able to support herself and her child. She wants her to have a better chance at life than she did. Knowing Michelle was having thoughts of sexual activity and she was dating, Tracy tightened up on Michelle when it came to her and her boyfriend spending time together. When they were at the house, no doors were allowed to be closed, no lights turned off, no movies or mall trips unless either parent drove; they can only visit each other if parents are home and they speak with each other before hand.

Michelle's high school love life was miserable. Her friends nicknamed her mother, "The Old Ball & Chain." They would argue at times, because she felt like she had no privacy, which was really, sexual frustration. Tracy knew, because she remembered how she was at her age; she was the same way.

So she allowed her to blow off steam, because she knew it wasn't personal, just puberty. Michelle would hear from her best friend, Kim, about how cool her mother is with her and her boyfriend. How she's allows them to be in the room alone, sleep over, go out on late night dates, as long as she calls and stays in contact, she trusted her. Kim caught an STD; that's how her mother found out she was sexually active. Since then, she has been on the pill, and her mother buys her condoms. Her mother's approach is much more relaxed than Michelle's mom. Kim's mom views it like this… why bother to stop her, she's going to do it anyway. When Kim's mom was young, she was the same way, and that's how Kim got here.

Things remained tense in the house until January of her senior year and graduation a few months away. Michelle and Kim recently received their acceptance letters from Florida University. Kim had also received a partial academic scholarship because she had a 3.8, not bad for a girl who is sexually active, has free rain, contracted an STD and has a hella cool mom. Two weeks into the 3rd Quarter of their senior year, Kim finds out that she is 2 months pregnant. She paid it no mind when she missed her period, because it happens from time to time since she started on the pill. Kim and her boyfriend used condoms on and off and never had an issue before. Kim has to change her college plans, just until the baby's born, and then she is off to Florida. The girls planned to room together during the spring semester.

Months pass after graduation and the girls lose touch a bit, but it wasn't an issue; they understood college was demanding. Michelle returned home for Winter break before the spring semester started in March. Excited to be rooming with her high school home girl, she comes home unannounced to surprise her. She goes straight to her house, rings the doorbell and her mother answers, excited to see her and to hear that she is doing well. Then, she delivered some shocking news about Kim; she has moved into her own place with her boyfriend and is doing well. Her mother gave her the address, they made more small talk and she left.

THE REALIZATION

Michelle arrives at Kim's house and knocks on the door. So excited to see her, she jumps through the door and hugs her and both girls scream at the top of their lungs. As the excitement starts to ware down, Michelle starts to focus on Kim and their surroundings. She notices that Kim looked like she has been putting on some weight, they always liked to work out together in high school and Michelle continued to do so in college. She makes a joke about her weight and says, "the first order of business on campus is to get Kim a personal trainer to tighten her back up." Kim pauses for a second after the comment, because it was at that moment that she realized, she was supposed to be going back to school with Michelle and being her roommate for the spring semester. The sudden silence caught the attention of Michelle and she knew that by the way Kim looked that something was very wrong. Then Kim reveals that she's pregnant again and that her and her boyfriend had to drop out of community college to help support the family. As they continued to talk about what has been going on with her, Michelle noticed that Kim's whole life is different now. She's a mother and has different priorities in life now and, unfortunately, education is going to have to take a back seat until later.

After about two hours of talking, catching up and crying; both tears of joy and sadness Michelle leaves. As she's driving home, things start to settle in with her about the choices that she has made in life related to the ones Kim has made and why they are in the situations that they are in today. The first thing that comes to mind is, "The Old Ball and Chain." She thinks about how she used to get so upset with her mother about privacy, boyfriend stuff, and started to understand that her mother was protecting her. Protecting her from falling short and not being able to have a full chance to develop as a young adult and get a good start at making a life for herself. She was not trying to deprive her of anything like she use to think, but teaching her about the importance of giving yourself a chance in life. Michelle entered her driveway with a newfound respect for her mother, herself, and her education. She's experienced a lot in the last few hours. When she entered the house, her mother was in the kitchen fixing something to drink. She walked up to her, gave her a big hug and said, thank you so much for being my "Ball and Chain."

THE CONCLUSION

I end this chapter with my argument that **Time** and **Attitude** are the key factors in parenting which determine whether parents fall into the "**Engaged**" or "**Disengaged**" category of parenting. Values and morals are things that are instilled in you by the people who raise you as a young person and support you primarily in life. Those adults in that process need to have developed over **"Time"** the appropriate **"Attitude"** to be able to recognize teaching moments and have the ability to turn those moments into life changing lessons, like Michelle's mother did. If those pieces are not in place or at their strength, then those adults in your support system must know that and create the proper supportive environment for you to develop appropriately. The mission in parenting is to create change by allowing chance. Giving your children the chance to reach the level you could not! To do this, as parents, we must be attentive, involved, understanding, clear about things, hold yourselves accountable, hold your children accountable and be the bad guy when you need to be, not a friend!

CHAPTER ASSIGNMENT:

Objective: To support positive youth development and productive parent (adult) engagement.

Goal: Parental awareness is just as important, if not more, than anything when discussing child development. Knowing your strengths and weaknesses as a parent are essential so you know when to seek support for you and your child when facing certain things in life. As parents, experience is a valuable tool—use it, whether bad or good, as teaching points.

Assignment: Part A) List the area(s) you lacked support in as a child that you wish you had more support in as a child and why you wanted that support or felt like you did not get it. Describe how not having the support you needed in these areas effected your development as a child, in both a positive and negative ways. Part B) Create a "Time Capsule." Write a support statement for your child (or youth you work with) explain how you will support them with more support than you had throughout your own life. Check it once every two years, review your progress in a journal, and see how you do.

Feedback: Email all questions and feedback to <u>Reasonswhyyouthdontgiveadamn@gmail.com.</u>

BARRY WOODS

Things young people need to understand… the hard facts about life!

» Don't allow your emotions to cloud your real issues.
» Adults may attempt to manipulate you if you try to expose them, unless you have video or audio, you will lose big! Get a trusted adult involved.
» The "Do as I say, not as I do," mentality really exist.
» Society really doesn't care! If you are not prepared for life, society looks for the next in-line.

CHAPTER FOUR

F@#K SCHOOL!!

The new mentality of today's, disengaged students and why they say we do not help.

"FUCK SCHOOL!"... IS the attitude of the young people struggling to get ahead or, "get a fair shake," as they see it in the game of life. Mainly, because the school system is not set up to support them, only to maintain them. In other words, do just enough so it can't be said that they aren't doing anything. The system of education does not even see its own value. Disregard the old age belief that, "children are our future", because whenever budget cuts are made, education seems to be the most expendable! To add more insult to injury alternative programing takes the biggest hit. You would assume that the support of disengaged young people would be a priority. Supporting alternative programing for disengaged young people helps to reduce crime rates by helping them develop into positive and productive members of society. When we cut funding for these kinds of programs, we do just the opposite. We increase crime rates and take away from society by adding one more inefficient individual. Lastly, I will discuss the teacher student relationship and how teachers need to be trained in a different manner to deal with today's young people. Teachers need to be able to understand the social emotional component that is attached to the profile of today's young people. Adults working with young people need to be able to determine that what they see from young people (through behaviors) lines up with effects of their home life, teacher relationships, peer relationships and how they (the teachers) impact today's young people attitude toward education. It should be mandatory for educators to receive Kinship training to understand the foundational support system that a young person has, or does not have to better support their development process. (https://www.researchgate. net/publication/327048486_The_Kinship_Model_Theory)

THE SYSTEM:

The last time I checked, school was about educating young people so they can become productive members of adult society. To **"EDUCATE,"** per the Webster Dictionary is to develop the knowledge, skill, or character by formal schooling (to teach). The process of education; teaching. As educators, our job is to **"EDUCATE!"** It is not to pass or push along the student who can't read because they're likable, or the parents present a challenge in meetings, or they're the classic natural terror or, "pain in the ass." No! No one with a mindset like that should call themselves and educator. Nor should they allow an uneducated student to move on to become someone else's problem next year.

Between grades, six and eight are key years of development for young people. During these years, they develop their **"SWAG"**, their personal attitude about life, how they view themselves and fit in with their peers. This starts to build up their personal, **"STATUS BAR"**, and influences how they start to prioritize things in life, and education. How we see **"PUSHING ALONG"** young people through their education as being beneficial, really boggles my mind. **EDUCATION IS TO BE EARNED NOT GIVEN!** It is the job of the educator to educate! Yes, a struggling student may be a challenge but to push them along is borderline criminal in my eyes. As educators we must be solution based and go the extra mile at times, which might mean going outside your contract to give a young person the true support they need.

It's proven from past research that behavior has a direct effect on the ability of a young person to be educated. I have seen adult ACES scores that are off the charts, so I could imagine a young person's score! If you can't focus as an adult, what makes you think that a young person can! It's hard to go to work and do your daily duties when you're unfocused, upset with your boss, co-workers or struggling with heavy personal issues. So, if it is an issue for us adults at times, how do you think a young person feels? On the other hand, what makes you think that they don't go through the same thing, something similar, or worse?

Yeah, I hear the peanut gallery in the background saying the following; there is not enough time to be the teacher, therapist and mentor, nor are you paid enough to do so and not to mention you have your own life, child/personal issues and family things to deal with. On the other hand, some of you might be saying why not pay teachers more money; add more classroom aides and social workers if needed. THESE ARE OUR YOUNG PEOPLE WE ARE TALKING ABOUT! We need to make sure we are preparing them the best we can for their future.

SCENARIO 1

Rahim is currently in the 7th grade and has been having a very trying time this year. Last year, in the 6th grade, he was so different. He was respectful, played nice with the other students, made an effort every day in the classroom and never did anything extreme. Teachers and students started noticing a change in him from the beginning of his 7th grade year.

The first few weeks of school teachers were complaining about his attitude and work effort in class. He was missing homework assignments, being kicked out of class for inappropriate behavior, negative outbursts in the classroom, and other students have reported him for bullying them during recess. By mid-year, he had already been suspended twice and had 10 detentions.

FOOD FOR THOUGHT?

Even though he had 10 detentions and was removed from class several times, his parent had only been called in for a meeting once, which was after the second suspension. No home visits were made by school social workers or anything. The normal response of parents and guardians of young people at-risk is not to get involved, to avoid exposing their own issues. Therefore, the effort has to come from the educator to identify and address these issues, or at least start the process.

As the year progressed, he continued to show the same behaviors and built a very negative perception for himself at school from both students and teachers. His mother was inconsistently visible at open house, progress report night; in addition, parent conferences always had to be adjusted due to her part-time work schedule, court dates, state appointments, groups and therapy sessions. Therefore, there was very little contact made by her or the school and the school didn't go overboard trying to reach her because she rarely responded anyway.

One day Rahim beat up a 6th grade student in the bathroom and stole his iPhone and sneakers. The student was hurt pretty bad; his eye was black and blue and he was bleeding from his mouth. The janitor found the boy in the bathroom and notified the principal right away! The principal brought the boy to the school nurse. He then notified the police, as well as his parents, and placed the school on lockdown. They originally assumed that someone had entered the school and violently mugged the student. In 40 minutes, police, news media, parents and family members surrounded the whole school. It was a zoo! All students were being escorted back to their homerooms during this time. After the 6th grader was cleaned up, checked by the nurse and paramedics and calmed down by his parents, he was able to tell the principal and police what had happened. After being locked down for the past two hours, the police and principal walked to Rahim's homeroom. Before entering, they spotted him through the glass. He was nodding his head to the iPhone and replacing the laces on the sneakers he just stole, while looking out the window staring into a daze

THE AFTERMATH

Rahim was sent to detention while the Department of Child Protective Services and the school social worker did a full investigation of his home life. They discovered that Rahim's father was killed last summer in a night club shooting. Since his father's death, his mother has been really stressed, depressed and started smoking dust (PCP). She lost her job and began prostituting out of their apartment to pay bills and support her drug habit. Rahim has seen his mother beaten by strange men and he, himself, has even been hit when trying to come to his mother's aid.

WHAT'S GOING THROUGH RAHIM'S MIND

He starts school as normal because it's routine and he gets to get away from the house. Once responsibilities like homework and studying for tests and quizzes begin, that's when his attitude shifts. ***Inside Rahim's Head: "Fuck this school shit man! Teachers with this homework and test bullshit! How the hell they expect me to remember to study and do homework when I don't know if I'm going to eat tonight. Or if my mom is going to either get killed or OD tonight. Man they buggin...FUCK SCHOOL! They don't give a damn anyway ...they have no idea what it's like to be me!"***

SCENARIO 2

Mark is in the 8th grade this year and is preparing to enter high school next year. From the start of the school year, he has been excited about going to high school. He talks about going to college with his parents, friends, and even teachers at times. His parents and friends both get as excited as he does when discussing his future. Mark has always wanted to become an accountant, and his teachers always told him he was good with counting money, so that motivated him even more. As the year came to an end, Mark and the other 8th graders took the high school placement test. A month after the test, students met with their guidance counselors to pick the classes for their freshmen year. Mark could not understand why he was being placed in resource for math and English. A few weeks pass by, but the buzz is still in the air for the 8th graders, with graduation nearing and high school schedules arriving home in the mail.

One day during lunch, he was talking to a friend whose mother is a high school teacher and he asked him, "What does it mean when you have resource math or English?" His friend responded, "That means you are in bone head classes because teachers feel that you can't handle the class work. Those are like the stupid classes, with like two or three students in your class. You can't even get into college taking those classes in high school."

During the remaining weeks of school, all hell broke loose. There were pranks, disrespect towards teachers, fights, and Mark played a major role in all of them. This is also where his negative attitude about education started to develop. Mark ended his middle school career on a sour note and carried that same poor attitude into high school. Needless to say, he really struggled; he refused to attend math and English on a daily basis unless his schedule was changed, which never happened! His frustration with school started to turn into anger about life. He just didn't have the skill and was refusing the help that would help him develop that skill. By his sophomore year, his anger had turned to hate for the school system, teachers and former students he used to be friends with. He felt like an outcast. By the start of his junior year, he was so far behind that he barely had enough credits to be a freshman at the age of 18. This presents another issue, because, legally, he can't be in classes with students under the age of 16. Over the next two years, Mark was placed in an alternative program with other students like him and graduated on time with his class. That summer Mark did not attempt to go to college, his whole outlook about his life and education changed after his freshmen year in high school. He had trouble filling out applications and completing entry exams during job interviews, because he was only at a 5th grade reading, writing and math level. Mark continued to struggle to find work and started to feel the pressure from his family as well about what his plans would be after graduation. Overtime he started to feel hopeless. Unable to find work or get into any community colleges or training programs due to being under educated, he started to try and, "Get Money" in other ways with his friends. Three weeks later Mark was arrested on a home invasion charge. The house they attempted to rob just so happened to be the home of his middle school English teacher.

HOW DO THINGS GET THIS FAR?

The scenarios above are far too common in today's world, but the question is, **HOW DO THINGS GET THIS FAR?** Why do students like Mark have such a struggle to receive the proper education they need? Why don't students like Rahim get the proper support? How do we, as educators and adults in these young peoples' lives, allow them to leave high school without the basic skills, so they have a chance to be successful in life? How do we as social workers, guidance counselors, mentors and life coaches over look or not notice the signs of an at risk young person? What really goes on at parent teacher conferences? Are teachers being forthcoming with all information, no matter how hard it may be to discuss with a parent? Or, are things being overlooked and by passed to avoid the confrontations that may happen if they are addressed? Are parents too busy? Are we, as parents, being mindful of the development of our own children; or, are we just washing our hands of it and saying, "the schools need to handle this?" Are we, as parents, too self-centered? Do parents need more support with their children? Especially single parents! Are they aware of resources provided to them: after school programs, local community center information, counseling resources, local and state assisting programs?

HARD FACT: Many parents have children at a young age and never get to complete their childhood and certain stages of development that they need to get through before becoming a responsible adult. This affects their ability to be effective parents.

Again, I go back to the importance of having appropriate funding for alternative school programing. Students like Rahim and Mark are becoming more common in today's world. Being able to support the social emotional needs of students like Rahim and Mark should be a priority in today's education system. Students like them need a program that gives them a combination of life skills and academics, along with some exposure to service learning and vocational programs.

THE BREAK DOWN OF ACCOUNTABILITY

There are three things responsible for this common form of poor youth development that we are seeing in today's society: 1) Teachers 2) Parents and 3) the System. All three are supposed to help support the development of our youth so they become productive members of society. Are they doing that? Well, here is how I see it from my experiences, and I'm going to start with the group that has the least level of responsibility.

Teachers

We have the good ones and the bad ones, and we all know it! There are teachers who pick-and-choose just like kids do. While a student picking and choosing may hurt your feelings or make you upset, when adults start picking and choosing as educators, we have to remember what we do affects the development of a young person. Yes, adults have the same hurt feeling and attitude of being upset; the difference is that, we have a direct effect on students' current lives and future. Teachers cannot operate with a disengaged or spiteful mindset! Yeah, it's tough being a teacher; you're not always appreciated by students, parents, administration and other staff. As a "Teacher," you are very, if not the most important, even though you may have the least accountability. How you ask? Because you have to produce the finished product! This needs to be a collective effort! **EVERYONE MUST BUY INTO A COMMON GOAL AND THE PROCESS OR APPROACH USED TO REACH THAT COMMON GOAL!** *This means the system has to be flexible in order to help the teachers support students correctly. Young people spend more time with educators than they do their own parents during critical years of development. On average, educators interact with young people 5.5 hrs. per day. In a world where both parents work and single parents work two jobs, teachers often spend more time with children than those who share the same living space. Who do you think has more overall influence on young peoples' development?*

The System

Or, should I say, "The people sitting in the offices downtown that have all the answers, but don't spend time with the people doing the work or in the schools to understand what's going on and what's really needed.

The two things really causing "The System," to remain this way are **EGO'S** *and* **BONUSES!** *Oops, did I say that! Yes, I did!*

Let's be honest people. Everyone at the **"TOP"** *wants to be the,* **"TOP DOG,"** *the one who gets all the credit and the* **"BIG BONUS"** *at the end of the year. What they need to be doing is, hiring more specialist and teachers to support certain situations. Be more supportive by taking a teacher's, or teachers' team, suggestions for a school and really applying them, regardless of who came up with the idea. So what, if it goes against your district plan! I thought it was about what's best for the students, the young minds that you are responsible for shaping for the future of our nation? It seems that more decisions are being made for personal gain at the "TOP" then for the future of our youth.*

Parents

Or should I say the, ***VICTIMS, THE CRY BABY, THE UNAWARE OR THE SHOCKED ONES!*** ***GET OFF YOUR ASS AND GET INVOLVED! THIS IS YOUR CHILD!*** *Ask questions, review report cards not just the one at the end of the year to see if they passed all 4 quarters. Sit down and check your child's homework, give a pop quiz once in a while. Let your child know you're interested in their education through your actions. Make sure your child is receiving all extra help and resource support available so that they can have the best chance of being successful by being fully prepared. This is why I hold parents the most accountable, because there is* ***NO EXCUSE*** *for you not to know what's going on with your child's education. Who gives a damn if you're tired and just getting home from a hard day's work? That's what you're supposed to do. You are the adult, right? The provider, the bread winner, you're supposed to work hard to support your family, that's a normal thing nothing special!* ***GET YOUR ASS UP AND CHECKIN WITH YOUR CHILD ABOUT THEIR DAY!*** *Attend the Open House school night so you can meet the teachers and know who is teaching your child. Exchange contact information, ask them to contact you about any issues. If things don't make sense, don't accept them until they do make sense. Don't be so trusting or gullible! I'm not saying not to trust your child; but, wait until they are out of your household. What is the old saying, "Only trust them," as far as you can throw them", translated into layman's terms,* ***"PARENT FOLLOW-UP."*** *Don't be a sucker just because you want to have a trusting relationship with your child. We all do! As a parent, that is the ultimate dream! Having a child who tells you the truth every time and respects your every wish with no issue; but, in reality, we know that's not true. Even little white lies count as being dishonest; all young people try to get over at times. Yes, even yours!*

REALITY CHECK

Now, I know a lot of you are thinking, "Well what about the young people? They have a responsibility, too. They need to apply themselves, maintain their behavior, complete their assignments, and ask for help when needed. Us parents can't do the work for them, nor can we make choices for them. They know right from wrong! I tell my child all the time how important education is to life, but they don't listen! Yes, today's young people are a handful more than ever to deal with, but this doesn't just happen overnight. It's the result of a time period full of neglect, not being engaged, a lack of lived experiences and not having your priorities in line. **IF YOU ALLOW YOUR CHILD TO GRADUATE HIGH SCHOOL UNPREPARED, THAT IS YOUR FAULT AS AN ADULT!** A parent being invested in their children's education is priceless!

PARENT DEDICATION TO YOUTH EDUCATION QUIZ

Below is a series of questions for parents to determine your investment in the support of your child's education. You need to be **100% HONEST WITH YOURSELF,** or it's pointless for you to even waste your time doing the quiz. That being said, all serious adults willing to accept accountability for their actions, get yourself a journal, go to a quiet corner somewhere, and take this quiz. The answers to this quiz will show you how truly involved you are or are not with your child's education. Take a minute and reflect on these answers, then sit with your child and develop and plan to either support them better or continue the support already being received. The average school year is about 10 months long, so every 3 to 4 months, go back to your journal and quiz yourself again so you can stay sharp. I mean, what's the worst thing that could happen? You and your child will form a better relationship, your child will feel better and do better at school because they feel supported and, "God forbid," they graduate and go on to college or trade school and become successful! Why? **BECAUSE YOU STARTED TO BECOME AN ENGAGED PARENT!**

PARENT'S DEDICATION TO EDUCATION QUIZ

BEFORE YOU POINT THE FINGER, SEE HOW INVESTED YOU ARE...

1. *How many times a week do you review and discuss homework and school with your child?*
2. *How often do you communicate with your child's teachers?*
3. *Do you understand the scoring scale with standardized testing?*
4. *Have you discussed the importance of the scores with your child's teacher?*
5. *How many books a month do you and your child read individually or together?*
6. *What is your child's attitude about school?*
7. *What is your attitude about school?*
8. *What's the last essay or book report your child wrote and was graded on, that you have read or reviewed?*
9. *When was the last time you helped your child with a book report or essay they had to write?*
10. *What math is your child studying now?*
11. *When was the last time you did some math problems or even reviewed some math work completed by your child?*
12. *Do you know your child's reading level?*
13. *When was the last time you heard your child read?*
14. *Is your child involved in school clubs, sports, after school programs and activities? Which ones?*
15. *How many times a year have you supported your child by attending school clubs, sport or out of school activities? If you didn't, what was more important? LIST IT!!!*

NOTE: *Parents should take this quiz each quarter during the school year and record your answers. If your answers don't improve over time, then you need to become more involved in your child's education.*

CHAPTER FIVE

"IT'S MY WORLD…YOU'RE JUST A SQUIRREL TRYING TO GET A NUT!!!"

Peer Pressure, Gangs, and Authority Figures

YOUNG PEOPLE TODAY have several reasons for showing certain behaviors. The issues arise when adults try to understand these reasons. One of the main ways adults trigger behaviors from young people is by trying to develop an understanding of the young persons' struggles and/or challenges. If the understanding that the young person has developed doesn't agree with our own personal or the collective principles and values of other adults—we don't respect it! That's where we go wrong. Regardless of whether or not we agree, as adults, we have to respect what young people see as their reality and meet them where they are. What we also have to understand is that times are different now! **BEEF!** Is not what it was in 1985, or even in the early 90's. Popularity, status, loyalty, money, power, and respect are real and are key elements that mold the egos, lifestyles and behaviors that we see from young people today. Think about it, threatening statements made by young people today towards adults are taken very seriously. If a young person says something crazy, cops are called, parents are called, schools are locked down or evacuated, meetings are called and plans are discussed to support the young person and their family. Now, if adults are reacting to statements made by a young person with such urgency, what makes you think the young person themselves wouldn't react with the same urgency when threating statements are made to them by other peers?

Gangs are the invisible, but very visible, enemy that we see our young people facing today more than ever (or should I say more than people like to admit). Gangs are the **ghost** of every community, who always seem to be the most visible in the schools and communities that **don't** have them! I hate to be the bearer of bad news, but gangs are here and they effect all of us: Black, White, Latino, Mexican, Chinese, Albanian, whatever! This gang thing is very real, and it's eating our young like Hannibal Lector! So we ask ourselves, why do young people flock to gangs? They know right from wrong. They understand that the gang life is full of struggles, pain and failure, right? WRONG…WRONG…WAY WRONG!

Gangs give young people the feeling that they belong to something and are accepted as a part of something like a family. The gang mentality is all about supporting and protecting their own. They have cool nicknames, handshakes, and through hand signals to communicate with their own members and at times too disrespect members of rival gangs. They identify themselves with colors and start fashion trends with their style, which affects how young people view their status and popularity in today's world. The most attractive factor for young people when it comes to being involved with gangs is, "The Tough Guy Badge," this adds to the invincible teen mind set. Overall, gangs give young people a feeling of respect, love, power, and family. These are the very things young people struggle to get from home, school, and society.

So, what do we do about the gangs and the influence they have on our young people and their education? Do we gather all the students in school who fit the criteria of a "Gang Involved Youth" and kick them out?

Or, maybe place them in remedial alternative programs with mediocre and non-caring teachers who will just push them through? Well, that's exactly what's been going on, and all it's doing is repeating the cycle! This cycle has been producing young people who's future revolves around a life of crime, making choices that lands them in and out of jail, unemployed, under employed, unemployable, under educated, unable to contribute to society in a positive manner, in a local cemetery or in the neighborhood on the celebrated and respected R.I.P mural.

I have a question… Has anyone ever thought about really working with and educating our at-risk youth? I'm talking about working with them afterschool, trying to find vocational interest for those not interested in college, college or even doing a home visit to gain an understanding of what they go home to everyday. Show an interest in their life outside of school. Their lives are different than ours. For example, some teachers are in by 7:15 and gone by 2:45 pm. "Students, if you need extra help, I come in at 7:00 am on Wednesdays." Instead, step outside the box, make a home visit, or spend extra time after school. This can open up different avenues and ways to connect and engage young people who might be dealing with struggles in the home, school, and their community.

WHY DON'T WE TEACH THEM? WHY DO WE ALLOW AT-RISK YOUNG PEOPLE TO CONTINUE TO JUST GO THROUGH THE MOTIONS AND BE PUSHED ALONG? WHY ALLOW THEM TO CONTINUE TO MAKE MISTAKES UNTIL THEY DIG A WHOLE FOR THEMSELVES TOO DEEP TO GET OUT OF? ARE OUR STRUGGLING YOUNG PEOPLE EXPENDABLE, OR JUST VIEWED AS SUCH?

First of all, if you're an adult and you "Fear" a student for any reason and you work in the school system you are in the wrong profession! THE FIELD OF EDUCATION IS NOT FOR PUSH OVERS! Therefore, if your attitude is such and you're in the field of education, why don't you just push on over and allow someone in who's going to teach! To those out there just working for a paycheck, take a leave of absence and have a substitute take your class for the year. At least they will be more vested in the young people's education then you. If you think that young people don't know your true intentions, you are wrong! They can smell bullshit from a mile away!!

Something to think about: *As educators we are quick to sit back and say, "I told you this student was going to turn out like that," or, "I saw this coming since their freshmen year." There are only two legitimate reasons to why this is allowed; "Fear" and "Teachers working in the system just to get a pay check."* (See the table on Page 57 Traits & Characteristics Of Teachers Who Are Misguided).

Another trigger that influences negative behavior in young people is peer pressure. Peer pressure today is nothing like it was in the early 90's or mid 80's. You just can't avoid things in today's world of Texting, Sexting, YouTube, Twitter, Snap Chat, Instagram, TikTok, and Facebook. Believe it or not, likes, dislikes, and texts being left on read are enough to really push a young person to suicide. Cyber bullies and email thugs are really going hard these days and the effect that they have on today's young people is crazy. As adults and educators, we need to understand this world so we can work with and around it to continue to help young people succeed. We must understand that today's peer pressure situations are not just idol threats or kids being kids, THEY ARE REAL!! Just because you haven't experienced it before doesn't mean it doesn't or won't happen. Sometimes, or should I say, most of the time, it happens and it's totally unexpected.

SCENARIO

Billy has always been the quiet one in school, accepted by everyone because he was an athlete, popular with the girls and a solid B+ student. During the summer of his 8th grade year, Billy started dating this young girl named Tanya. Tanya was a 2nd year sophomore, but the hottest girl in high school, who also used to date Mark. Mark was going into his senior year and was a talented baseball player but known to be a hot head. Tanya had a reputation of being a drama queen, always looking for a stage and willing to put on a show. When Tanya and Billy started dating, she was still dating Mark; however, by the end of the summer, Tanya had chosen Billy over Mark. Mark was devastated, not just because he was cheated on, but because he lost his girl to an underclassman. The news spread like wildfire. Once, Tanya updated her Facebook status with a new picture of her and Billy, along with a few embarrassing details for Mark. Mark was upset but cool at first. It wasn't the first time he was dumped, and he was cheating, so he kind of understood the game. Once his friends heard the word that Billy was a freshman, the pressure was on...

> ## WHAT WAS GOING THROUGH MARK'S MIND
>
> Damn... This shit is crazy right now... I'm not even really sweating this chick or the situation, but I'm not about to allow this silly ass freshman to play me out like this. My boys are clowning me! I'm not about to be made a fool of during my senior year. I might just have to whip this little freshmen dude's ass on the first day to set the tone THAT I'M NOT TO BE FUCKED WITH !!!!

By the first day of school, the tension in the air was so high, Mark couldn't go one minute without someone making a comment or joking about it indirectly. They would normally ride the same bus, but because it was the first day, Billy's mother dropped him off. Billy also doesn't have a cellphone or computer at home and being that he was an 8th grader last year, was not really too big on the Facebook thing yet. So he was coming to school totally unaware of the extra tension that had been brewing because of Tanya's Facebook comment. I mean, he knew about Mark and was aware of him being upset over the summer, but thought he had moved on. Secondly, he's a senior, about to graduate, why would he risk it over a girl?

For the entire 20 minute bus ride, Mark's boys are hyping up the situation. Telling him how Billy has been talking about him, clowning him and telling people how he took his girl. I mean, they had Mark so heated on the bus he almost got into a fight with his best friend. By the time, the bus pulled up to the schools courtyard, Mark was seeing RED!

Mark exits the bus with a mob at his back making a "V-Line" for the freshmen wing of the school. Billy is at his locker with a few friends, excited about their first day. They are comparing class schedules to what classes they may have together and what lunch wave they have. Out of nowhere, Mark spins him around and slams him against the lockers. Mark ends up putting Billy in a coma, which later resulted in him eventually passing away from brain damage. Now Mark is on trial for murder and looking at spending his life in jail.

<u>CONCLUSION</u>

Situations like the scenario mentioned above happen all over the world on a daily basis (Columbine High School, Sandy Hook, and the Virginia Tech Shooting to name a few). As adults and educators, we need to listen and take heed to the feelings of our young people. We must also understand that today's young people are most influenced by their own peers. Some young parents have been known to put their own children second for the satisfaction of their peers.

This is why proper communication with our young people is important on all levels: school, home, and community. These circles of support must communicate with each other, putting the best interest of the young person first. Remember, they are the one who have to continue to live through the change you just implemented in their life. Shouldn't they have a say? Wouldn't you want to have input on your life that held value and could impact your future? Oh wait, you have that, you're an adult. So I guess a young person's voice doesn't count. Hopefully, this is a common thing we can start to change. Our young people are our future, their voices should matter!!!

Thank you for your time. I hope you enjoyed this reading and will put some ideas mentioned to use to help support the young people of today with proper development. With support, young people can continue to make a positive impact on our society and send the same positive message to the next generation.

TRAITS & CHARACTERISTICS OF TEACHERS WHO ARE MISGUIDED

TEACHERS IN EDUCATION WITH ULTERIOR MOTIVES: MONEY, AUTHORITY & CONTROL

1. They are only available for students during working hours, meaning scheduled appointment (usually during hours that are not realistic for students) and never any after school time, unless they are being paid.
2. Very reluctant to go beyond the basic norm and usually has one of the two types of attitudes: a) "I only do what I get paid for." b) "If it's not in my contract, I'm not doing it."
3. Makes hurtful statements to and around students, such as, "I get paid whether you pass or fail."
4. Does everything they need to do so they stay under the radar and are not confronted by administration.
5. They have more of a dictatorship style classroom environment vs the recommended democratic engaging style classroom environment, which is much more effective.
6. Is usually spiteful with discipline and other actions, will go as far as taking it out on students academically, and holds grudges against students.
7. Does not ask to have parent meetings outside of Back to School Night, Report Card Night, and Parent/Teacher Conferences.

TEACHERS WITH NO CONFIDENCE OR TEACHING OUT OF FEAR

1. Trying to be too much of a friend or the cool teacher.
2. Is nervous about assigning detentions, sending students to the office, and supporting suspension offenses.
3. Shies away from dealing with the most challenging students and allows them to dictate the flow of the class.
4. Has a very hard time trying to establish ground rules and usually never does, which results in a carefree class environment. This results in the teacher only teaching students who come to learn and not reach to the students who need to learn.
5. Has no classroom control: *students talk out of turn, leave the room when they choose, and pay attention when they choose to.*
6. Has no respect from the students in their classroom or in the school.
7. Has a very hard time giving any type of direction or discipline.

A Letter from The Author

IDID NOT WRITE this book for public approval of any sort. My main purpose was to expose the things I have seen during my life and my experience working with young people that go against the motto of our society that "Children Are Our Future." ***Reasons Why Youth Don't Give A Damn Anymore*** is not written for the soft hearted, or the person who acknowledges these issues behind closed doors and does nothing about them. It was actually written to expose people like you and others in positions of authority who have a direct impact on the development of young people. So, if you don't agree with my views and get offended by things I'm saying…GOOD! Now that puts you in one of two positions: to do something about it or accept that maybe you're part of the problem!!!

We need to stop looking for our own gratification when giving young people guidance about life. Supporting young people is what we are supposed to do! Make a positive impact, be a role model, but it's not a competition. Young people are not pawns to get grants! It's just like in the streets, your big homies are supposed to look out for you and guide you so you don't get bagged by the cops or caught slipping by your enemies. That is what's needed from educators, community members, mentors, and parents to give that proper guidance and let it go. Don't get caught up looking for the thank you or the pat on the back right away; it will come but over time, sometimes years. So don't make that a reason or a driving force behind anything you do with, or for, young people. We must remember it's not about being the most popular it's about being the most respected, not feared, respected. Respect, is the one thing that will speak for itself, whether the young person does or not, because it will show through their actions.

The crazy thing is that if your goal is really to support the young people (and not support yourself through supporting young people), then you will agree with a lot of the things I have written, but will you do something about it? Just agreeing or saying, "Man he keeps it so real!" is not enough! You have to put things into action by either changing the things you do or supporting change in some way. If you're not doing that, then you're just blending in with masses and clearing your conscience by acknowledging what's right but saying it's out of your hands. It is **not** out of your hands – no matter what you do, where you live, or the lifestyle you keep, today's youth need your guidance. Be a part of the solution!

Respectfully Yours
Mr. Woods

How to develop and improve your relationship with young people:

» Give up control! Take away every option from the young person to rebel. Then restate each thing you did to give them control.
  - Example: Young person says, "Leave me alone and I'll be quiet and work." The adult should back off and allow them 3 strikes. If the young person becomes disruptive or gets off task in anyway, then engage.
  - Explain to them the responsibilities that you both have in this process and how you both must hold each other accountable, which at times is going to become uncomfortable, but we have to make sure we're doing our part.
  - If they don't become disruptive and they honor their words with actions, acknowledge that. Call them over and let them know you respect them for keeping their word and you're proud of them.
  - Effect: You just made a deposit into their *emotional piggy bank!* Everyone likes to be acknowledged!

62   BARRY WOODS

How to develop and improve your relationship with young people:

» When you make a mistake that hurts a young person, own the fact that you were wrong, and you made a mistake. Be sure you let them know you apologize. Whether they accept your apology or not at that moment is not the concern. They have to hear you apologize, the conversations may resonate later.

» If a young person is right when calling you out on a negative behavior, accept and acknowledge it: don't try and cover it up.

Printed in the United States
by Baker & Taylor Publisher Services